Parcel

A Play

David Campton

A Samuel French Acting Edition

FOUNDED 1830

SAMUELFRENCH.COM
SAMUELFRENCH-LONDON.CO.UK

Copyright © 1979 by David Campton
All Rights Reserved
Insert Art Credit Here

PARCEL is fully protected under the copyright laws of the United States of America, the British Commonwealth, including Canada, and all other countries of the Copyright Union. All rights, including professional and amateur stage productions, recitation, lecturing, public reading, motion picture, radio broadcasting, television and the rights of translation into foreign languages are strictly reserved.

ISBN 978-0-573-12196-8

www.SamuelFrench.com
www.SamuelFrench-London.co.uk

For Production Enquiries

United States and Canada
Info@SamuelFrench.com
1-866-598-8449

United Kingdom and Europe
Theatre@SamuelFrench-London.co.uk
020-7255-4302

Each title is subject to availability from Samuel French, depending upon country of performance. Please be aware that *PARCEL* may not be licensed by Samuel French in your territory. Professional and amateur producers should contact the nearest Samuel French office or licensing partner to verify availability.

CAUTION: Professional and amateur producers are hereby warned that *PARCEL* is subject to a licensing fee. Publication of this play does not imply availability for performance. Both amateurs and professionals considering a production are strongly advised to apply to Samuel French before starting rehearsals, advertising, or booking a theatre. A licensing fee must be paid whether the title is presented for charity or gain and whether or not admission is charged. Professional/Stock licensing fees are quoted upon application to Samuel French.

No one shall make any changes in this title for the purpose of production. No part of this book may be reproduced, stored in a retrieval system, or transmitted in any form, by any means, now known or yet to be invented, including mechanical, electronic, photocopying, recording, videotaping, or otherwise, without the prior written permission of the publisher. No one shall upload this title, or part of this title, to any social media websites.

For all enquiries regarding motion picture, television, and other media rights, please contact Samuel French.

MUSIC USE NOTE

Licensees are solely responsible for obtaining formal written permission from copyright owners to use copyrighted music in the performance of this play and are strongly cautioned to do so. If no such permission is obtained by the licensee, then the licensee must use only original music that the licensee owns and controls. Licensees are solely responsible and liable for all music clearances and shall indemnify the copyright owners of the play(s) and their licensing agent, Samuel French, against any costs, expenses, losses and liabilities arising from the use of music by licensees. Please contact the appropriate music licensing authority in your territory for the rights to any incidental music.

IMPORTANT BILLING AND CREDIT REQUIREMENTS

If you have obtained performance rights to this title, please refer to your licensing agreement for important billing and credit requirements.

CHARACTERS

Grandma
Rose
Amelia
Arthur
Bus Conductor
Man (or **Woman**) in buffet
Policeman (or **Policewoman**)
Passengers
Customers

The action takes place in a living-room, on a bus, in a bus refreshment room, a street, a police station, a bus station.

Time—the present

PRODUCTION NOTE

Although indications of the setting are given to locate each scene, the production should flow as smoothly as possible. A permanent setting has been devised with this objective in mind, with lighting to suggest changes of time and place. However, there are many other ways of staging the play: the well-equipped might indulge in flown scenery, back projection, or even a revolving stage! I hope producers will feel free to exercise their ingenuity.

There is wide scope for improvisation among the supporting cast. The Passengers on the bus need not remain mute—so long as their dialogue does not swamp that with the Conductor.

The Customers entering the refreshment room can be any group of human beings—football supporters, a wedding party, or merely people changing buses. Although in the early stages of rehearsal maximum freedom should be given to actors to develop characters, motivation and business, in performance the movement and dialogue of the Customers will need to be carefully orchestrated to give the impression of business as usual without distracting from the scene between Rose and Arthur.

Although the dialogue is comic, care should be taken not to lose sight of the fact that the characters are real people who can be hurt and bewildered. The play is a comedy—with undertones of debate on the function of the Welfare State—and not a light entertainment script.

PARCEL

A living-room

On the sideboard lie a long scarf and a small case

Arthur, wearing hat and coat, is trying to fasten the case. Grandma sits with her back to the audience. Rose and Amelia enter. Rose is dressed for outdoors and carries a balaclava helmet. Amelia carries hat, coat and gloves

Rose Will she need her balaclava helmet?
Amelia It keeps out the cold, doesn't it? When you get to her age you want the cold keeping out.
Rose That's right, isn't it, Grandma? Of course it is. Let the cold in, and you never know where it's going to strike.

Rose drops the balaclava into Grandma's lap. In none of her questions to Grandma does she expect an answer, and so never waits for one

Amelia You know she's back in flannelette nighties.
Rose Flannelette's a comfort when the nights are drawing in, isn't it, Grandma? You know it is. Haven't you done that case up yet, Arthur?
Arthur It's done.
Rose Then we're all ready.
Amelia *She's* not.
Rose Haven't you got your balaclava on yet, dear? Don't just sit there holding it. (*She fits the balaclava on to Grandma*). Your head goes in here, and your face sticks out here. Don't worry about your hair. We'll comb it when we get home.
Amelia It's a new hat.
Rose Oh, isn't that nice, Grandma? A new hat. You'll like that, won't you? Yes, you will. (*She takes the hat from Amelia and puts it on Grandma*)
Amelia I threw the old one out. The moths got in.
Rose It suits you, doesn't it, dear? A nice new hat.
Amelia Oh, I almost forgot. I've taken her off the milk stout.

Rose But she's fond of milk stout.
Amelia It gives her wind.
Arthur Nothing like a glass of milk stout and a packet of crisps.
Amelia We put a stop to the crisps long ago. We won't talk about what crisps did to her. When you get to her age, your inside's not what it was.
Arthur Where's the harm in milk stout?
Amelia Don't you give her ideas. I know what's best for her, thank you.
Rose Melia knows best, Arthur.
Arthur Of course Amelia knows best.
Amelia After a milk stout she'd sit there burping to herself for hours.
Arthur She needs something to pass the time.
Amelia You're not complaining about what I've done for her, are you, Arthur?
Rose Of course he isn't. Grandma's very thankful for what we do for her, aren't you, dear? Of course she is.

Amelia puts the coat on Grandma and buttons it up. It fits the old lady from head to foot. This process takes place during the following speeches.

Amelia I put the telly on every night.
Rose That's nice, isn't it?
Amelia She sits right in front of the set from six 'til eleven. News. Quizzes. Westerns. There she sits.
Arthur With her eyes shut.
Amelia She likes it that way. She watches telly with her eyes shut, because she's used to the wireless.
Arthur She always used to be on the go. Hadn't you, old dear? Jamming, bottling, whitewashing, bricklaying ... If it wasn't one activity, it was another.
Amelia When you get to her age, activity is something you can well do without. When you get to her age, rest and comfort are what you need. And a good nurse.
Rose She has good nurses, haven't you, Grandma? Rose and Melia.
Arthur I didn't hear her answer.
Rose My goodness, you're in a mood tonight, Arthur. She

appreciates what Melia does for her, don't you, dear? And now you're coming to stay with Rose.

Arthur Then let's get started.

Rose (*stepping back to admire*) And she's got a new coat, too.

Amelia Hardly used. Old Mrs Gormley's. They buried her last week. Old age, you know. Just old age. But she wasn't looked after. Not the way Grandma's looked after.

Arthur It's on the big side.

Amelia Rose has got the machine. She can take a foot or so off the bottom.

Rose It covers her beautifully. It'll keep the night air out, won't it, dear? And gloves. You'll need your woolly gloves, won't you?

Rose helps the old lady into one glove, and Amelia helps with the other

We'll help you on with them. This little piggy went to market. This little piggy stayed at home. This little piggy... That's right. Now the scarf. The scarf, Arthur!

Arthur hands the scarf to Rose

Thank you. Round and round we go.

Rose winds the scarf round and round Grandma. There is now nothing to be seen of the old lady but her eyes

Arthur Like a parcel.

Rose Just like a parcel. A cosy old parcel. Now we're all ready. Say good-bye to Melia, Grandma. We'll see her again in three months. Oh, by the way, what did you give her instead of milk stout and crisps?

Amelia Arrowroot.

Rose Arrowroot, eh? She'll like that, won't you, Grandma? Good-bye, Melia.

Amelia Good-bye, Rose.

Arthur Good-bye.

Still saying "Good-bye" Rose, Amelia and Arthur go out R with Grandma L

A bus interior

Passengers enter L and seat themselves. Arthur, Rose and Grandma enter and sit nearest the exit. The Bus Conductor enters and takes fares, coming to Arthur last

Arthur Three to the bus station.

Rose You've got your bag, have you, Grandma? That's right. Hold it tight.

Conductor You want to hold the tickets, love? (*He gives the tickets to Grandma*)

Rose That's right, Grandma. You hold the tickets. It gives her something to do, doesn't it? You like to have something to do, don't you, dear? That's right. She's a lovely old person.

The Conductor stands by the seat, swaying slightly with the motion of the bus

Conductor You're a lovely old person, are you, Gran?

Rose Oh, she's a lovely old soul. You wouldn't know she was in the house.

Conductor Haven't got much to say for yourself, have you, Gran?

Rose And clean.

Conductor That's nice.

Rose Like a new pin, aren't you, Grandma? And appreciative. I've never heard her utter one word of complaint.

Conductor She can talk, can she?

Rose Talk? She used to sing soprano.

Conductor You were a singer, were you, Gran?

Rose Sing? You should have heard her belting into "The Holy City". Shouldn't he, Gran? He should have heard you in the old days. I was only a girl at the time, but I remember "The Holy City". And "Thora". And "Home, Sweet Home". With variations. She doesn't sing now, of course. It's her age.

Arthur And losing the piano.

Rose Arthur!

Arthur I only said ...

Rose We heard what you said. The way he goes on about that piano. You'd think it was his.

Arthur You didn't have to break it up. I did.

Rose Half the notes were stuck, and the other half were out of tune. The piano tuner wouldn't look at it. He'd go sick every time we asked him to call round. Anyway, she couldn't drag a piano around with her. You'd look fine trying to get a piano on a bus. Once every three months . . . She sold up, you know. It was the best thing to do. She couldn't go on living alone for ever, could she? I mean, she was past it. She wanted looking after. Lucky for her she had those who could look after her.

Conductor They look after you, do they, Gran?

Rose Oh, she's looked after all right. Me and my sister—we share her. Well, it breaks the burden, doesn't it? And it makes a nice change for her. Three months in town, and three months in the country. You like the country, don't you, Grandma? Fresh air. Very good for old persons.

Arthur So she sold up.

Rose Arthur!

Arthur I only said she sold up.

Rose You needn't sound so awkward about it. He's like this every time we fetch the old lady. It was the best thing to do. You can't hang on to old pianos all your life, can you? It's not as if they're worth anything. The man only gave a pound for her mahogany sideboard—not a scratch on it and you could see your face in the polish: but there's no call for them. Who wants a mahogany sideboard these days? Anyway, she kept her special little bits and pieces. She carries them in her handbag. And she doesn't complain.

Conductor Not the complaining sort, are you, Gran?

Rose She eats everything you put in front of her—stew, semolina, slippery elm—it's all the same to her. No left-overs. And she does as she's told.

Conductor Do as you're told, do you, Gran?

Rose You've only got to say "Bedtime", and off she toddles. No trouble at all.

Conductor You're a good girl, Gran.

Rose We're taking her home with us now.

Conductor Bus station next stop.

The Conductor exits

A bell tings. The bus stops

The Passengers get up and crowd into the exit in front of Arthur, Rose and Grandma. By the time they have all gone Arthur, Rose and Grandma have gone too

A bus station refreshment room

An attendant enters and stands behind the counter. Arthur, Rose and Grandma enter L

Arthur (*gloomily*) Half-an-hour.
Rose Here's a table. (*She seats Grandma at the table*)
Arthur Half-an-hour.
Rose I don't run the buses. It's not my fault if ours goes without us. Think ourselves lucky we're in a refreshment room. At least we're under cover 'til the next bus comes.
Arthur Half-an-hour.
Rose We'll be able to swallow a cup of tea without choking ourselves. You'd like a cup of tea, wouldn't you, Grandma? Of course you would.
Arthur She'd like a milk stout.
Rose She's having a cup of tea. That's three cups of tea.
Arthur I'm having beans on toast.
Rose You surely don't want beans on toast.
Arthur After tea at Melia's I could eat anything. What about you?
Rose Well, if you're making a hog of yourself, I'll have a ham sandwich.
Arthur A ham sandwich.
Rose No, I won't. I'll have a bun. With icing on top. If it's lemon icing.
Arthur A bun.
Rose No, I won't. I'll have a meat pie.
Arthur You're sure it's a meat pie you want?
Rose And a packet of crisps.
Arthur Meat pie and a packet of crisps. And a packet for her?
Rose Not for her, Arthur. Not crisps.
Arthur She likes crisps.
Rose You know what crisps do to her.
Arthur What's one packet more or less?
Rose She is not allowed crisps.
Arthur They're only potatoes.
Rose You're not arguing, are you, Arthur? Crisps are not good for her. So no crisps. Thin arrowroot biscuits, yes; crisps, no. You'd like a thin arrowroot biscuit, wouldn't you, Grandma? Of course you would. Bring a thin arrowroot biscuit, Arthur.
Arthur You can carry the biscuits.

Rose Me?
Arthur I'll need help. I can't carry three cups of tea, beans on toast, meat pie, crisps *and* a thin arrowroot biscuit. Not with only two hands.
Rose Helpless! Leave your hat on the seat. We don't want anybody bagging our table. If you don't look sharp, you won't have time for beans on toast . . .

Arthur puts his hat on a seat. He and Rose cross to the buffet

A party of Customers enters, arguing. They pause in front of Grandma's table. When they have finished arguing, some, including The Man, go to the counter, some find seats, and some go out. When they move away, Grandma has gone

Rose and Arthur return from the counter, with three cups of tea; and a plate of beans on toast, one of a meat pie and crisps, and an arrowroot biscuit

Of course you would have to insist on beans on toast. You might have known you'd have to wait for the toast. Which is our table?
Arthur There's my hat.
Rose Are you sure?
Arthur It's my hat all right.
Rose It doesn't look like our table.
Arthur I remember the dent.
Rose Something's missing.
Arthur Put your tea down. You're slopping.
Rose I don't want to put my tea down on somebody else's table.
Arthur Let me recognize my own hat, Rose.
Rose Well, if this is our table, where's Grandma?
Arthur Grandma?
Rose We left her here, didn't we? We sat her down before we went for the tea.
Arthur So we did.
Rose If we put her there, she ought to be there now.
Arthur Are you sure this is our table?
Rose There's your hat.
Arthur I could have been mistaken.
Rose I remember the dent.
Arthur But if that's my hat, where's Grandma?

Rose She's gone.
Arthur Gone?
Rose I said gone. There's a space where we left her. Gone.
Arthur Do put your tea down before you drop it.
Rose Where is she?
Arthur Perhaps she's slipped under the table.
Rose Don't talk daft. Have a look.
Arthur Me?
Rose We want to be sure, don't we? We want to be sure she's not under the table before we raise an alarm.
Arthur You're not going to raise an alarm, Rose. (*He looks under the table*)
Rose Is she there?
Arthur No.
Rose Well, then.
Arthur She must be somewhere. She couldn't just disappear. She was too solid. To say nothing of Mrs Gormley's coat, and her balaclava.
Rose But she's not here.

Arthur sits at the table

Rose You're not sitting down, Arthur.
Arthur My beans are getting cold.
Rose You're not touching a bean 'til we find her.
Arthur Drink your tea. She'll have gone for a walk.
Rose Walk? I'd sooner expect the chairs to walk.
Arthur Perhaps she's moved to another table.
Rose It takes initiative to move to another table. What would Grandma want with initative? She was looked after. She was satisfied.
Arthur Don't fret so. Nobody's stolen her. Who'd want her?
Rose She'd no right to go missing without warning. She'd no right.
Arthur Did we leave her on the bus?
Rose Don't be silly. I was talking to her. I wouldn't talk to her if we'd left her on the bus. Would I?
Arthur Pity. If we'd left her on the bus, we could have picked her up at the Lost Property Office.
Rose Arthur! You were joking.
Arthur I can make a joke, can't I?

Rose Not here. Not now. Stand up and look round. You couldn't miss an old lady in a balaclava. Nobody could. Can you see her?
Arthur No.
Rose Where could she have gone?
Arthur There are places.
Rose She went there before we started. Everything was done for her that had to be done. She was looked after.
Arthur Better check.
Rose But you're not stuffing yourself on beans while I've gone. You can be asking.
Arthur Asking? Asking who? Asking what?
Rose Anybody. Everybody. Somebody's bound to have spotted her. Ask which way she went.
Arthur But ...
Rose Ask, Arthur. Ask.
Arthur But, I'm ...
Rose When I get back, I'll expect you to have asked.

Rose exits

Arthur Oh—fiddle! (*He gets up, goes to the counter, and taps the shoulder of the Man standing there*) Excuse me.
Man Yes?
Arthur Have you seen an old lady.
Man Me?
Arthur An old lady.
Man What about her?
Arthur Have you seen her.
Man Where?
Arthur Anywhere.
Man (*considering*) An old lady.
Arthur My wife's grandmother. Have you seen her?
Man Do I know her?
Arthur You'd know if you'd seen her.
Man Why?
Arthur She's an old lady.
Man (*ponderously*) Your wife's grandmother.
Arthur That's right.
Man (*thinking*) Have I seen her.
Arthur Yes.

Man No.
Arthur You haven't?
Man Yes. I haven't.

Arthur turns away and accosts various customers

Arthur Excuse me. I'm looking for an old lady. She was sitting there in a balaclava helmet, with a new hat and a handbag on her knee. She was at that table, facing you, so you couldn't have missed her, could you? I mean, if she'd moved, you'd have noticed, wouldn't you? So I was wondering if you had. Noticed.

The answer is a shake of the head, so he tries again

Excuse me. I wonder if you could help. Has an old lady in a balaclava helmet passed this way? We left her alone, turned our backs, and . . .

The look of blank incomprehension deters him from going on. He tries another, as he bumps into her

Excuse me . . .

But it is the returning Rose

Rose Granted. Oh, it's you. She's not there.
Arthur She's not here, either.
Rose Arthur . . .
Arthur We've lost her.
Rose We shouldn't have left her. You wouldn't leave a parcel about like that. Anybody might come along and pick it up.
Arthur Nobody's picked her up.
Rose How do you know? Much you know. Much you care. You and your beans on toast. If we hadn't waited for that, we'd never have lost her.
Arthur If you hadn't insisted on meat pie and crisps, you could have stayed with her.
Rose I could have stayed if she hadn't wanted arrowroot biscuits. But you put yourself out and this is your thanks. If we hadn't fetched her a cup of tea, we'd never have lost her.
Arthur If we'd never brought her, we'd never have lost her.
Rose Arthur, you're not being difficult again.
Arthur I always said these three-month swaps were a mistake.

Parcel

There was bound to be an accident sooner or later. It stands to reason. Keep shunting anything backwards and forwards long enough, and you're asking for breakages. Pots, tomatoes or old ladies, it's all the same. I always said she should stay in one place. But no—Arthur's being difficult again.

Rose What should have been done then?

Arthur We should have left her where she was.

Rose At Melia's?

Arthur Farther back—with her mahogany sideboard, and her wax fruit, and her old piano.

Rose We did what was best for her. We've always done what was best for her.

Arthur Have we?

Rose We should have gone by train.

Arthur Eh?

Rose She couldn't have gone far if we'd come by train. If we'd been on a station, she'd have been stopped at the barrier. At least we'd have known where to look.

Arthur We couldn't have come by train. They closed the line.

Rose I didn't vote for it.

Arthur You're not yourself, Rose.

Rose I'm upset.

Arthur I'm upset, too. Does that make you feel better?

Rose I feel so—empty-handed.

The Man approaches with an old umbrella

Man Excuse me, did you say you'd lost an umbrella?

Rose We've lost my grandmother.

The Man considers the object in his hand

Man No. This is an umbrella. Sorry.

The Man exits with the umbrella

Rose What are we going to tell Melia?

Arthur Melia?

Rose We can't tell her we've lost Grandma. You know Melia—everything in that house is tagged and labelled. Not a pin out of place.

Arthur I never cared much for Melia's place.

Rose I was always the careless one. Buttons, handkerchiefs,

stockings, bags... They were always getting away from me. Melia never loses a thing. And she knows it.
Arthur She has other faults.
Rose She'll never let us forget. She'll rub it in. "Remember the time you lost Grandma", she'll say.
Arthur But she'll laugh when she says it.
Rose Whether she laughs or not, it's a nasty thing to say. You know Melia. "I've known you to lose things in your time," she'll say, "But Grandma...!"
Arthur She's not lost. Only mislaid.
Rose Next time I mislay anything she'll say "Like Grandma".
Arthur She had to go some time.
Rose But it's not as if she'd passed on. She's walked off. You know Melia. She'll go on rubbing it in. She'll never let us forget.
Arthur Then we shan't tell Melia.
Rose She'll ask. Oh, what are we going to do?
Arthur Find Grandma.
Rose How?
Arthur Look.
Rose Where?
Arthur Out there.
Rose Out there?
Arthur If she's not in here.
Rose But there's so much of—out there.
Arthur Come on. (*He picks up his hat and Grandma's case*)

Rose goes with him. By the exit Arthur bends down and picks up a battered object

Arthur Hey—what's this?
Rose It's her hat. It's been trodden on.
Arthur Or jumped on.
Rose Trodden on.
Arthur Kicked about.
Rose Trodden on.
Arthur Trodden on.
Rose She dropped it.
Arthur She trod on it.
Rose What does it mean?
Arthur She must be out there.

Rose How do we start looking in the dark? There are at least six ways out of the bus station.
Arthur Better try them all. You take one, and I'll take another. And call.
Rose Call?
Arthur Grandma.
Rose Grandma?
Arthur (*calling*) Grandma!
Rose (*calling*) Grandma!

Rose and Arthur exit, calling

The Lights fade to a Black-out

The Attendant and Customers exit

A street

The Lights fade up. Arthur and Rose enter from opposite sides, calling

Rose Grandma.
Arthur Grandma.
Rose Grandma?
Arthur No, it's me. Any sign?
Rose The only shape like hers was a pillar box.
Arthur She must have moved fast.
Rose What do we do now?
Arthur Carry on looking.
Rose We'll miss the bus.
Arthur We can't go without her. Anyway, there'll be another bus. There's one every hour until the last.
Rose What does she think she's doing, the crazy old thing?
Arthur That's a good question. Put yourself in her place.
Rose If I were in her place, I'd know where she was.
Arthur She might have gone into a pub for a milk stout.
Rose (*calling*) Grandma!
Arthur She was very partial to milk stout.
Rose (*calling*) Are you there?
Arthur And arrowroot's not the same.
Rose (*calling*) Grandma!
Arthur Serve it how you like, you'll never give arrowroot the appeal of milk stout.

Rose Can you hear me?
Arthur She might have been attacked by a sudden hankering.
Rose (*calling*) Grandma!
Arthur She had money of her own, you know. Fifty pence a week. And it didn't all go on peppermints.
Rose Grandma, where are you?
Arthur She could be in a pub. But there are so many.
Rose She only had to stay put while we collected her.
Arthur Perhaps she felt it didn't matter where she was. Like thistledown.
Rose Like what?
Arthur Or an old bus ticket, blown about.
Rose Have you gone potty, too?
Arthur Or a dried leaf. It doesn't matter where a dried leaf comes to rest. It doesn't belong anywhere.
Rose You agreed. Melia agreed. I agreed. She agreed. She was past living on her own. "Sell up," we suggested, and she didn't say no. There'd been accidents. She couldn't light a fire or boil a kettle without risking life and limb. What would the neighbours have said if she'd blown the house up, or set fire to the street? You have to think about others in this world. She just couldn't have gone on at Slater Street.
Arthur That's where I'd go, if I were her. I'd go back to Slater Street. I'd go back to the bit that was mine—even if the lavatory was at the end of the yard, and you shared the entry with four other houses. Only she couldn't have gone back to Slater Street. Nobody could. There is no Slater Street now. They've done away with it.
Rose They've no consideration.
Arthur They had no choice, I suppose.
Rose They get past considering anybody but themselves.
Arthur There's nothing left.
Rose Their own convenience—that's all that matters to them.
Arthur Their what?
Rose Their own convenience.
Arthur Then they should have stayed with it. But they all went. She wasn't the only one. They all gave in. Now what's left for them?
Rose I want. I want. That's them.
Arthur Windows boarded and the roofs off.

Parcel

Rose My goodness, there's a rude awakening coming for some of them.
Arthur Not just pianos and sideboards. The floorboards have gone. They've all moved. All of them. The street's gone.
Rose Where would she be without us now, eh? Where would she be?
Arthur Perhaps they gave up too easily. But she can't have gone back to Slater Street, wherever she's gone.
Rose Wherever she is, she's not thinking about us.
Arthur If we can't find her on our own, there's only one place to go.
Rose Where?
Arthur The police.

Arthur exits

Rose The police? Not the police, Arthur. Not the police.

Rose exits

A police station

A Policeman enters with a large ledger. He stands behind the counter. Arthur and Rose enter furtively. They go up to the counter. Arthur whispers into the Policeman's ear. The Policeman whispers back. Arthur whispers again

Policeman A bit more information, sir, would be a help. To put it crudely, information is the life-blood of our business.
Arthur We lost her at the bus station.
Policeman That's a start.
Arthur In the refreshment room.
Policeman Ah. (*Writing*) The—refreshment—room.
Arthur Fourth table on the right as you go in—the one next to the window, facing the door marked "Private". There's a crack in the table top. And there's a mark on the wall behind it as though somebody had thrown a cup of cocoa at it. Or it might have been soup. Above that there's a picture of a girl in a bathing-suit with a fizzy drink. There's a word pencilled across her bathing-suit. I couldn't read it, though, because I was too far away.
Policeman That's the refreshment room, sir.

Arthur Yes. That's the refreshment room.
Policeman But you didn't lose the refreshment room.
Arthur No.
Policeman Then a bit more, sir, about your particular loss.
Rose She was ungrateful.
Policeman (*writing*) Ungrateful... Age, for instance. And colouring.
Arthur Well, she was old. And white. What you could see of her.
Policeman Anything else?
Rose Ungrateful.
Policeman Height, weight and suchlike commonplace details.
Arthur Height and weight?
Policeman She has height and weight. Everybody has.
Arthur We didn't have her weighed and measured.
Policeman An oversight.
Arthur We didn't expect to lose her.
Policeman Nobody expects to lose anything. Did you lock the door before you left home? Are all your windows fastened? Are you insured against burglary?
Arthur No.
Policeman You neglect elementary precautions and then complain... Any scars, birthmarks, or other distinguishing features?
Arthur Me?
Policeman Your property.
Arthur She had—er...
Policeman Yes?
Arthur Well, she had—she had a face.
Policeman Most of them do. With eyes, nose and mouth in the usual places?
Arthur Yes.
Rose There was ingratitude written all over that face.
Policeman I'll make a note of it.
Rose Black ingratitude.
Policeman (*writing*) Black.
Rose Ingratitude.
Policeman (*writing*) Ingratitude. Any special idiosyncracies?
Arthur Like what?
Policeman Was she fond of liquorice allsorts? Or cats? Was she given to sunbathing or cold baths?

Arthur She was an old lady.
Policeman So you said. But did she collect things—butterflies, stamps, matchboxes, bottle tops?
Arthur I didn't notice.
Policeman Did she talk to strangers? What were her religious inclinations?
Arthur How should I know?
Policeman What made her different from a million other old ladies?
Arthur I don't know. I'd know her if I saw her again.
Policeman We can't set up a net, and sweep in the lot for you to sort through. What was she like?
Arthur I tell you I don't know. She was there—then she wasn't. That's all.
Policeman That's all.
Rose She was ungrateful.
Policeman I did make a note of it.
Rose Where would she have been without us?
Policeman That's a different question. You wanted to know where she is now.
Rose If it wasn't for us, she'd have gone the same way as that piano.
Policeman Piano? You lost a piano as well?
Arthur It was worn out. I broke it up.
Policeman Then you're not worried about that piano.
Arthur Not often.
Rose It was an act of charity. Pure charity. She'd no claim on us. We picked her up out of goodness, and looked after her out of the kindness of our hearts. You could preach sermons on what we did for her. We provided her with a chair and a bed. Complete with all furnishings. Oh, yes, we supplied cushions and hot-water bottles, too. Every comfort. "That's comfortable, isn't it?" I'd say. And it was. We found her in bedsocks and slippers. And food. Only what was best for her went in. Our digestions had to struggle with pies and crisps, but she had arrowroot, and malt extract, and cod liver oil. Her pension didn't cover the cost of keeping her, and she knew it. It hardly paid for her rubbing oils. And let me tell you, it's not everybody who'd put up with the smell of wintergreen soaking into the curtains. I tell you some days it was so bad I daren't strike a

match. That's charity for you. Pure charity. Well, we'll hear a different tune from now on. Another smack in the eye like this, and it's the old persons' home. She'll notice the difference there. She should have been grateful. That's what I can't get over. The ingratitude.
Policeman If you did so much for her, why did she go?
Rose Did you have to ask that?
Policeman It's all information.
Rose You think we're at fault.
Policeman I don't think. I collect information. One old lady lost. That's all.
Arthur This is her hat. (*He puts it on the counter*)

The Policeman pokes it with his pen

Policeman A hat?
Arthur Hers.
Policeman If we find her, we'll see if it fits. Bring it back with you.
Arthur If you find her?
Policeman We'll let you know. Or you can drop in from time to time. Not too frequently, of course. We do have other duties.
Arthur Come on, Rose.
Rose But we haven't ... She's still ... We don't know.
Arthur We'll have to catch that last bus. Come on.

Arthur and Rose go out. The Policeman watches them go, then makes a gesture of resignation to human folly, and goes out with the ledger

A bus station

Arthur and Rose enter L

Arthur Bus isn't in yet.
Rose That's what they'll all say, you know. "What didn't you do for her?" I don't know. What didn't we do, Arthur? What more could she have asked for?
Arthur Don't fret, love.
Rose We looked after her. We looked after everything.
Arthur Of course we did.
Rose It's turned cold.
Arthur Could be white over by morning.
Rose Cold as charity.

Arthur You never had that cup of tea. It'll be past drinking by now.
Rose We did our best. Nobody can say we didn't do our best.
Arthur Nobody, love.
Rose But they will. They'll say "If they did their best, why did she go?"
Arthur Don't you worry. You did your best.
Rose Then why did she go?
Arthur Come and have that cup of tea.
Rose And, Arthur...
Arthur If you don't stop needling yourself, you'll never sleep tonight.
Rose What *did* she look like?
Arthur Just like any other old lady. Except that she was wearing a balaclava helmet.
Rose Not much of a difference, is it—a balaclava helmet?
Arthur It's past, Rose.
Rose It's not. Oh—I could do with a cup of tea. What shall I do with her hat?
Arthur Hang on to it. You never know. It's bound to fit somebody. Come on.

Grandma enters, carrying an enormous bag of crisps. She stops on seeing Arthur and Rose

They'll soon be closing.
Rose Arthur—look!
Arthur There's a thing. Balaclava helmet and all.
Rose Eating crisps.
Arthur She must have been at it all night.

Grandma hastily stuffs the last of the crisps into her mouth

Rose Now she'll hear something.
Arthur Rose...
Rose And you stay out of it. I've something to get off my mind. (*To Grandma*) Now Grandma. I said, "Grandma"! If you'll just stop crunching for a minute and listen to me.

Grandma screws up the bag. Arthur takes it

Arthur Family size.
Rose You know what they do to you. We're in for a fine night.

Well, let that come when it may. Right now there's something you can tell me. Why? Eh? Why? (*Pause*) I don't understand. Why? Didn't we...? If it wasn't enough, what else...? (*Pause*) You were, weren't you? (*Pause*) There is nothing else, is there? (*Pause*) Why then? Why? Why?

Arthur We'd better get to the bus.

Rose Why?

Arthur It's nearly time.

Rose (*deflated*) I meant—why? (*Pause*) Put her hat on then. Keep the night air out. And brush those crumbs off her. There are bits of crisp all down her front. We don't want people thinking we don't look after her.

Rose jams the battered hat on to Grandma's head, and flicks the crumbs off her coat

There's a baked bean. And some flaky pastry. We'll have to get that lot moving. I'll give her a dose before she goes to bed. And we'll put her in the corner of the bus—next to where the baggage goes. Just in case of accidents.

Arthur You're all right, are you, Grandma?

Rose Of course she is. We look after you, don't we, Grandma? Of course we do. And you need looking after, don't you? Of course you do.

Rose continues to talk as she and Arthur escort Grandma away, and—

The CURTAIN *falls*

FURNITURE AND PROPERTY LIST

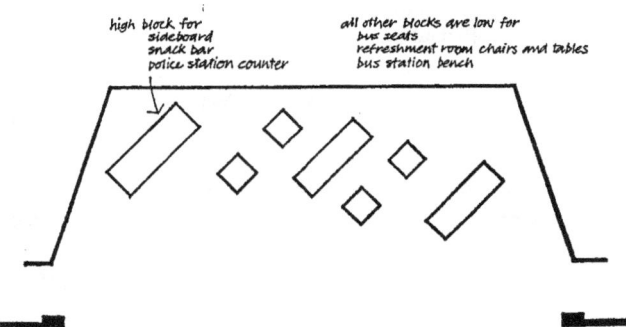

For furniture list see Production Note and set plan

LIVING-ROOM
Scarf } pre-set on sideboard
Small case

BUS INTERIOR
Tickets, satchel, coins (**Conductor**)

REFRESHMENT ROOM
3 cups of tea, saucers, teaspoons
Plate of beans on toast, knife, fork } pre-set behind counter
Plate of meat pie and crisps, knife, fork
Plate with arrowroot biscuit
Old umbrella (**Man**) (pre-set behind counter)
Grandma's hat, battered duplicate (pre-set, concealed, near exit)
Coins or note (**Arthur**)

POLICE STATION
Ledger, pen (**Policeman**)

BUS STATION
Large bag of crisps (**Grandma**)

LIGHTING PLOT

Property fittings required: nil
Various scenes in standing set

To open: Living-room lighting

Cue 1	**Rose, Amelia, Arthur** and **Grandma** exit *Cross-fade to Bus Interior lighting*	(Page 3)
Cue 2	On general exit from bus *Cross-fade to Refreshment Room lighting*	(Page 5)
Cue 3	**Rose** and **Arthur** exit *Fade to Black-out, then up to Street lighting*	(Page 13)
Cue 4	**Rose:** "Not the police." *Cross-fade to Police Station lighting*	(Page 15)
Cue 5	**Arthur** and **Rose** exit *Cross-fade to Bus Station lighting*	(Page 18)

EFFECTS PLOT

Cue 1	**Conductor** exits *Bus bell tings*	(Page 5)

www.ingramcontent.com/pod-product-compliance
Lightning Source LLC
Chambersburg PA
CBHW070456050426
42450CB00012B/3296